THEORY

OF

DEVOLUTION

D1472232

THEORY

OF

DEVOLUTION

David Groff

Poems by David Groff

University of Illinois Press

Urbana and Chicago

© 2002 by David Groff
All rights reserved
Manufactured in the United States of America
1 2 3 4 5 C P 5 4 3 2 1

♾ This book is printed on acid-free paper.

Library of Congress Cataloging-in-Publication Data
Groff, David.
Theory of devolution : poems / by David Groff.
p.   cm.
ISBN 0-252-02779-5 (cloth : alk. paper)
ISBN 0-252-07086-0 (pbk. : alk. paper)
I. Title.
PS3557.R538T48   2002
811'.54—dc21   2002000254

THE NATIONAL POETRY SERIES

The National Poetry Series was established in 1978 to ensure the publication of five poetry books annually through participating publishers. Publication is funded by the late James A. Michener, the Copernicus Society of America, Edward J. Piszek, the Lannan Foundation, the National Endowment for the Arts, and the Tiny Tiger Foundation.

2001 Competition Winners

Betsy Brown of Minnesota, *Year of Morphines*
Chosen by George Garrett; published by Louisiana State University Press

David Groff of New York, *Theory of Devolution*
Chosen by Mark Doty; published by the University of Illinois Press

Terrance Hayes of Pennsylvania, *Hip Logic*
Chosen by Cornelius Eady; published by Viking Penguin

Elizabeth Robinson of California, *Pure Descent*
Chosen by Fanny Howe; published by Sun & Moon Press

Ruth L. Schwartz of California, *Edgewater*
Chosen by Jane Hirshfield; published by HarperCollins Publishers

ACKNOWLEDGMENTS

The author gratefully acknowledges the editors of the following publications in which some of the poems herein first appeared, some in slightly different form:

American Poetry Review: "Birthing" and "Proving Ground"
The Chicago Review: "Leaving the Farm"
The Georgia Review: "The Crabmeat Pickers" (as "The Crab Pickers")
The Iowa Review: "Daisy Buchanan, 1985"
Mississippi Review: "Swing"
The North American Review: "The Saddle River"
Northwest Review: "Naming Constellations"
Poetry: "The Sense of Well-Being"
Poetry Northwest: "Memory" (as "The Memory") and "The Watchdyke"
Poets for Life: 76 Poets Respond to AIDS: "A Scene of the Crime"
Poz: "Fall"
Prairie Schooner: "Addison Groff Chooses the Ministry"
Selections: University and College Poetry Prizes: "For Catching Hardshell Crabs" (as "For Catching Crabs")

The author also wishes to thank Stephen Berg, Steven Cordova, Alfred Corn, Jan Crawford, Scott Hightower, Stephen Koch, Timothy Liu, Richard McCann, Marie Ponsot, Kelly Rowe, and writing group colleagues past and present.

For Clay Williams
and
for my mother and father

CONTENTS

ONE

THEORY OF DEVOLUTION

1

The studio apartment is emptied, it echoes;
the cat, hungry, is discovered, fed.
Dead, I become the common coin
dropped through a hole in my lover's pocket,
a clatter in the gutter of the city I love.

I pull the streets into myself.
I am the oil, screams, and debris,
the horns coughing,
the blond sun setting at the foot of 17th Street
that splatters Chelsea with matter.
Dusting the grayed department stores,
I am the lilt in the bantam Spanish,
the muscle of new construction.

2

A star the size of the sun exploded yesterday
150 light years ago or away.
Its hydrogen exhausted, it devolved,
the peony unpetaled over time.
It sent out only its neutrinos,
intangible as a smell,
particles so small they barrel through atoms.
I see neutrinos in the sun declining over Chelsea,
flamboyantly setting,
shouldering between the tenements,

a drag queen on her way to tea.
Compared to the whole of the star or the queen
I am very small, a single sequin.

3

Last night, twisted tight
in his wide arms,
I came, and it hurt bad,
the pleasure strung out of me
as a kind reminder of pain.
But for the first
time in many comings
I was only body,
a blaze of sensations,
sweat, summer heat,
the sum of the hairs
of our torsos and toes.
I looked into his eyes
and they were anybody's.
Gone was the net
of psychology, the grave
particulars of his history.
Instead, in the spray
of lines that graze his face
I read just exposure to the sun.
We lay like lizards.

4

If he was really Christ I pity Jesus—
drop-kicked into the afterlife,
denied a body his friends could prep for decay.
The movie star of spirits, he sped away,

limousined, not a contract player any more.
Better the Jesus who talked up the dying thieves,
the stress of the cross ripping his tendons apart,
screaming at God like a normal person.
Better the mother with a dying daughter
calmly planning dinner for the relatives.
Better to admire Len, whose body's rife with poisons
and his brain ablaze. Better to be here.

5

Under our sneakers the sand receded.
Len and I walked facing the sun
as the ocean did its usual thing,
commanding sand from the shore.
Len blinked a lot in the hard light.
His steps hurt both of us,
I thought he'd trip and not catch himself
and the water would pool around his neck and ears.
But he was nearly sand and ocean already
and knew it, I think, though he was quiet.
Dragging pain,
he treaded the tideline dividing
sand from sea, humans from clams.
He smiled as the water sucked.
Len eddied into ashes eight months ago.
I breathe, I take him in.

6

Lover, you hold me hard
as if I were the pope on a flying visit
or your last quarter.
You and I are animals rubbing each other,

grain against grain,
the bonus simply that we know we know our names,
the players in the Super Bowl, the resemblance
between sunset and drag queen.
The mind that asks specifics of the street,
the mind that giggles and grieves
is, like a comb, a necktie, a dishwasher,
pleasant to have but not
essential. What matters is matter.
Microscopic and huge, the lasting us
vaults beyond the sum of the city,
the postcard summer house, a spray of carnations,
the taste of your hair in my teeth.
Here with me, prepare with me,
prepare to fall with me, fall very far—
and so ascend like a sensible Jesus
into the element that blooms.
I feel your heart resound or tremble.
Oh, always-dying particular man,
your orgasm mustered in pain,
shred your drag and become some day with me
the exploding star.

LAST MOON

The milky egg of it bursts
from the horizon's uterine wall,
spraying its goblins of light
over the boyish ocean.
How could I ever turn from it
back to the beach house blaring
its spasms of television?
If my soul had smarts enough to focus,
if I kept looking for all time,
respected patience and paid
supreme attention, impaled
on discipline like a flagpoled monk,
I could hold it right there,
test-tube its preciousness,
intimidate carbon into diamond;
or more lively yet, let
the fossils and plant cellulose
lube the moment to eternal petroleum,
or proof it like a photo, its black colors
not a portrait but the face itself,
stayed by my chemical gaze.
Still you, mother moon,
my mother (let's get real),
your arteries narrowed with choices,
you of the gingered hair that streams with gray,
the Betty Grable grin that brims with gravity,

heave further above the fishing craft
no matter how deftly I loiter.
Bearing your stole of dowager's hump
you brave your powdered path
through the flashbulb mob of stars,
teasing waves your way
and smaller with each step.
Sand sandpapering my toes,
the sextant of my neck gets cricked.
Commerce tugs me inland.
As if you were childhood,
the friends in eighth grade made at last,
or the cracking of virginity,
I revolve to leave and let you rise and fall.
Time to go,
time for summer to windfall from the branch,
for the rental to lapse.

FALL

In New York's streets, summer's odors bloom again,
Streaking the air with piss, a season's worth
Of fatty suppers, and all the human oils.
Shirtless, reprieved, and eying each other,
The brave ones strut, risking pneumonia.

The doctors sent Marc home as almost bones.
His mind had flaked like summer skin,
Or, to be precise, the virus had blurred its distinction,
Stepping Indian file through the capillaries,
Scorching the brain's earth.

Half-blinded, he forgot the name of his disease
And lay in his bedroom, pale as sheets.
—That October afternoon, the heat intense,
He just strolled into the kitchen
Saying he was hungry. He conversed with you.

Was it the heat that made him so coherent,
Amused at your hair, so fakely blond?
And what exactly made him laugh,
Palms curled around a coffee cup? He was really beautiful,
The sun washing the hollows from his face.

Long since stripped of hope, stunned and afraid,
You carried his wheelchair to the roof
And sat him, wrapped in a quilt, by the ledge,

All of Chelsea just beyond his knees.
Then the wind picked up, men slid on their shirts,

Clouds sprawled across the sun, smells sank distinctly
Back into the pavement, and pigeons soared off the roof
Into the new rain. For him you fell away.
Marc smiled and smiled, his eyes all light.
The chair settled a little in the solidifying tar.

PROVING GROUND

John Vinsky lives just in a copper-colored picture
Dated *Bush River, 1939*, washed out over time;
Past his broad legs the water reads as air.
How many days or weeks was this
Before he left the river for cancer and Poland?
It hurt him to lift an oar. When John was harbormaster,
Says my father, the crabs almost leaped to your hands.
So my old man comes back every year
And stands there smiling, feet planted on the shells.

He hears the Aberdeen Proving Ground send
Dud missiles over the river's Chesapeake mouth,
A whine that scared off the bass, but he does stay.
Or he recedes to the night the family ate crabs
Cooked in the fire's ashes on the cottage lawn, when
Juny stepped grinning out of the darkness, home from the war,
Pulled his cousin my father to his feet, and hugged him—
Juny who died at sea that fall, to follow John Vinsky
Into the coppery glow my father allows in himself.

If he ever can make another life, if heaven
Can be sand, tidewater, pine roots tough enough
To creep almost to the docks, then my father
Will shed his shell to be Juny or John;

It doesn't matter which, as long as he comes back
A waterman, a sort of harbormaster,
On a tidal river, in a place that loves him.
John Vinsky thought of Poland that way
When he packed his bags in pain, in 1939.

A SCENE OF THE CRIME

Going home near dawn from the last great party
Of the '78 season, when Miss Fire Island
Got a long drugged kiss from a Perry Ellis model,
He hears behind a slatted wooden fence
The suction of two men fucking.
Their sweat seems to moisten the dry air.
The ocean mutters, the men mutter
And laugh, a rhinestone bracelet
Sails gleaming toward the stars
Like a falling star until it sinks
With a plop into the pool.
He stands transfixed, lonely, high,
Unable to muscle himself away,
Smoking one, two, three cigarettes, awaiting
The shrill orgasmic cry.
It comes, and then, "Bud, I love you, I love you!"
One, two bodies dive into the pool and make a single
Splash that causes him to love the whole idea of love.

He drops his cigarette, forgets to scratch it out,
And heads home to his rented bed
Drunk with other people's sex,
Aware in other rooms and other houses, in the wild,
Of the salty come-togethers of some thousand men.
This odd domestic life—greased by drugs and easy come,

Easy go—goes on, so naturally, so left alone.
Elsewhere, Sadat and Begin make their peace.
He falls asleep, glad for the flaming island.

Amazing how long a cigarette can burn.
Iran and Carter fall, Gloria bellows
At the island like a very mad contestant,
And late one night, right after Reagan gets his way,
In the driest leaves occurs the slyest arson:
An ember awakes to find itself a flame
And flames surprise themselves into a fire.
Above the brush, the boardwalk bursts
Into a hunger so fierce it seems years in the making.
It gobbles the dune to the door, unsated, until
The house is a swift-collapsing pile of smoke
And sparks dance electric from roof to roof;
Men who are seasoned but unprepared for fire
Scuttle from house after house that burns and burns.
They inhale the ash of poison ivy.

The following spring, with the world's little wars
Torching a hundred here, another dozen there,
But with the national economy still fairly firm,
On a day so great the deer emerge
To eat the holly berries and nose the surf,
The man who didn't mean to
Walks the boardwalk once again, in sunlight, older.
When he finds the house a mass of charred
Board and curtain rod and splintered glass
He breathes in hard and feels in his lungs
The stink of fire.
He recalls his smoke and chokes with guilt.
But he considers how many years have passed
Since the night he thought he fell in love with love.

He considers the usual comparison to AIDS
That sweeps his island like a fire,
An accident they seem to *breathe.*
At that moment on the island, in a thousand cities,
Another dozen soldiers drop like stars.
He feels the bullets strike between their shoulder blades
And hears the groans as they go down.
He lights a cigarette, blows out the match,
And, feeling singed, stares at the pool
Braceleted by cyclone fence,
A crater filled with water and ash.
He wonders if they were lovers. Did the lovers burn?

GLORIA

Odd the way she selected their ruin,
licking a finger, pressing it down,
in her airiness, to snap
a glass roof, split wood,
push pines across bedrooms—
and then excuse a vase,
unscathed on the sideboard,
as if the vase were her elect,
prearranged to stay, to show
her taste in placement;
as if any hurricane could choose
to pick out Curtis and leave Dave alone;
as if she herself could name
which bodies she'd impress
into the ocean, a tumult
of mustaches, deltoids,
and furious cries,
selecting the men to sail her ship
(men who happened to linger
curious at the dock too long)
and leaving their lovers behind
on the thinning shore—
breathless, only boyishly tousled,
who watch the pirate queen sail off
with all they thought they owned.

LAUGH

You must understand that what I say is false,
no more real or lasting than a licking flame.
That summer never was; the faces of Negroes
collapse like tinder.

In the summer heat of 1968
Quinn, a fireman, is drinking.
My parents' faces shine pink
on Quinn's glass porch. His wife
lies on the couch; she can stand
but cannot bend her back—an accident—
still she is cheery. I am ten,
my first beer finished and wet on my mouth.

One by one, Quinn says, they dragged out the blacks
from the fiery tenement, some of them shrieking
on the pavement, rolling themselves clean of flame.
When Quinn looked up, the water tower on the roof
lost a leg to flame and crashed, cooling everyone
who'd gathered curious, faces red with light.
Quinn found a man in a hallway, crouching,
his face bare of breath, his black skin blue.
He pulled the man by an arm down the stairs through the smoke
and outside in the pool of headlights
he put a mask against the man's nose and mouth.
It was as if the man was laughing,
his body gasping for air against the arms

that pinned him into safety, his eyes rolling
then staring out at all the white and fiery faces.
At last, like a split tire hissing air,
he shut his eyes and gave way.

It's not true they lifted off the mask and found him dead.
It's not true they'd never switched on oxygen
and they didn't carry him behind a screen of smoke
up the stairs to let him burn in someone's living room.

Quinn wipes his mouth and hands us all more beers.
I take another, but Quinn already swims in smoke.
I watch him glance at his wife whose head
lies cocked and smiling on its cushion.
She loves this man.
                              Quinn leans back
and takes the deepest breath I've ever seen. He laughs.
My father is laughing, my mother, my brother, me.
Would you have laughed, if you were white, or Quinn, or ten?
I've changed our names. The laugh is true.

PICTURE OF HEALTH

These are boys you couldn't nod hello to, Ron,
sauntering your streets, though they come with faces you knew
and bodies it's possible you borrowed for a night,
for thanks to the cocktail that confounds their virus
they are thickened and thinned past recognition:
their torsos swell with muscle and fluids,
but the bloodwork that bulges in their nodes
also planes fat from their faces,
your Chelsea a terrarium of cheekboned
lizards, their visages as knuckled as a fist,
the extra skin collapsed like swags around their lips;
they are raw with a brand of chemoed hopefulness
that—let's face it—you never knew,
your death so badly timed, your self tattooed with spots
in no design. They are pregnant with promise
as you were, but differently, when you were
a chorine fresh to town, your head fantastically blond.
Cocktail waiters every one,
their heads are prows,
leached, weathered wood,
the keels of their jaws quivering,
slicing the ozone as they steam ahead
of you, sickness at their sterns,

ships stripped for the trip.
Enough of comparisons
to inanimate things. Ron, it's an odd era
you'd give a ball or two to mingle in, when health
reads for all the world like death.

OLD PORNOGRAPHY

They straddle the fin of a Cadillac,
nibble a melanized rose,
or sprawl on the raw mattress
improbable in heels and plastic slacks,
their organic dyes flushed
to bruisy green, their blushes brown.
Their pouts by now all parody—
her hair so caustically teased,
his mustache silly even for a seal—
they slump beneath their legends:
"Nancy, an art student, frolics bravely
in the sylvan beauty of an Irvine orchard," or
"Derek takes pleasure in his own physique,
taut from years swabbing decks in the Navy!"

Their grins erotic as paper,
each tongue forever just about to prime
a lip as black as the vaseless rose,
the G-string guy keeps squinting at his staple,
the bride remains on hands and knees,
the nun half-lifts her rump from red bedclothes,
a cheerleader, standing, perpetually pees,
the roped kid holds his breath:
this petrified forest of desire

winks from its wilderness of time.
Their acid content high, their bindings rust,
these senior citizens who can't retire,
your consorts in the vegetable death,
beckon you to pulp, to eat their dust.

ADULTERY WITH JESSE GERSTEIN

Sly in his desire, he stared me down in the shower,
his ponytail a thinning corkscrew,
its sleek end-rope coy around his throat
and arrowed by the downgoing stream
to a groin that twitched like a vendor
with a watch inside his coat to sell.
We didn't have the time or place to do it.
We left the locker room to talk like breakfast friends.
Just a couple minutes were all he had.
By the time our bagels had gone to seeds
I had us rent-stabilized in Soho,
the minister's son and the adventuresome
Jewish New Yorker on his own since seventeen,
a photographer of objects for department stores:
We'd pose like sculpture for the shelter magazines.
I was too green to get he wanted only sex.
He could be wholly present with his coffee
yet hide his life inside his open eyes,
even breakfast probably an imposition.
We'd started naked, after all.
A night years later, haunting his address,
I was cornered by his grin outside his lobby door.
He wore trapezoidal spectacles, uneasy, pleased.
He made me linger in Korean deli glare downstairs
while he shot something brass for Bloomingdale's.
I slipped up to his loft, which was not in Soho.
He used a lambskin condom,

flourishing the square of it, a magic hankerchief.
It wasn't safe to do. The gut is porous.
It got late, the big windows flashing darkness.
"I'm starting to fade," he told me at last,
so he could conclude and get me to go.
His obit, placed by Jerome Robbins,
was terse with endearments.
Who knew? The gym went under,
its profit inhaled as cocaine, but reincarnated
under beefier management with fresh carpeting,
sleek machines, and a bright new name,
but the same historic shower tile.
It's possible the diner has been renovated too,
though it's as persistently vinyl as ever,
Harry Chapin wailing on the radio.
Jesse, you blink from today's bowl of oatmeal.
Which booth along this wall was it a thousand
men ago we occupied, wearing such natural skins?

SWING

Two grown men, men grown as I am,
play basketball one on one, giggling,
tripping and getting up fast
like children. The sun
glints in the sweat of their beards.
Eight times they miss before that orange ball
sinks with a cough through the chain net.
Strange, to call myself a man.
I sit on a swing, and when my hands reach out
from my sportsjacket pockets to grip the chain
I nearly fall, then
steady so I almost float, and swing
like the windy maple shadow I played with once
that caught my feet in its raised roots.
I think this swing is what I mean:
the way I fall back and forth,
how I darken and brighten the grass,
how the sun falls in and out of my eyes
the way it rubbed my leg in the maple
until I leap and land dizzy on the scraped earth
and the men on my right have gone, no longer play ball
like children, but children play ball on my left,
the limbs of their bicycles tangled on the grass.
The older brother, who's maybe eight, whose arm is
slung around his younger brother's shoulder,

tells him how to throw a ball—
bend your arm, then straighten out.
To swing from the ear.
The sun in our eyes says dinner, and across my legs
falls the brother-shadow, linked, at play.

THE GUY WITH THE BATHING SUIT
AROUND HIS NECK

In his severe tanness he dives,
wriggling into the wave
with his red necklace of Lycra,
all color compared to the blank foam,
his white butt twin fishes
twitching, and so defies
abrasion abrasion abrasion,
cruising into shore like driftwood,
his groin skimming the gutted shells
and sand whose breathing holes
are stops on the piccolo of beach;
not scraped too bad to quit this time,
not bloody,
(though through the salt-sting
can he tell what incises him?),
he scrambles to strut in again,
the ocean bullying
his breastplate of a body
into an eruption of spume,
butt-tumble, bald brown head,
a noose of scarlet,
and sky-pointed soles—
between his legs
the stream of micro-organism,
the scrotal gamble
with jellyfish, crab, cracked oyster,
the risk of scarification the risk

required to feel fetal and manly again,
to be held and to be witnessed from the shore,
such a big baby
no mother can pluck back home,
such a bad boy, bareback
on the ever-dissolving spine of sea.

RON DIES

Even in my deathbed I arouse you,
my gown undraping my incisioned chest,
its hairs a dust your hand would cause to rise.
All over I open up for you:
My penis cathetered
is more of a penis than ever before,
tethered as it is, a lion on a chain,
the organ we could never take for granted.
Oh, I see how you stroke me in my fever,
how you would drown your sorrows
in the shallow bowl of my breaths.
But mute as I become,
engorged with fluids, flat, absent of all
expression except my twisted harsh dismay,
all I truly am is body to you.
When I convulse at last
and devolve from dying into death
my body isn't pretty. In repose
(you ask why it's called *repose*)
my chin drops into my neck,
my bowels give way as bowels will do,
my eyes harden.
I go prematurely gray,
with every sense but sound reminding you
that I am matter. Go in peace.

TWO

LEAVING THE FARM

When I get sick of my own body
I become cousin Peter Hershey,
six and a half feet tall and sick of Pennsylvania,
walking down past the prairie and jungle to where
Teddy Roosevelt is building the Panama Canal.

The Mississippi's flooded but I step across
on tree limbs and the carcasses of horses.
The woman who watches gives me her mule
and I beat a cyclone into Mexico
where they've got a temple to some god
Mexicans fall down in front of, screaming,
waving their arms for its attention.
When I pick my way through, tall, a white man,
the plain goes silent.

In Panama they have to blast out mountains:
I go bent over into the caves with dynamite,
light the fuse with my cigar,
and push my way out just in time.
In one great burst, just like a bullet in the chest,
my mountains explode.

But I'm not made for any one place
and adventure is no warm stove.
I feel the old pull toward magnetic north;

before they lock the oceans together
I chuck my shovel. I walk back home.

On my father's farm at harvest
I step off the top of the wagon
into the hay binder.
                          That's one story
easy to believe. I keep seeing Peter
ease out on the conveyor belt,
six and a half feet of square red package.

NO ANSWERS FOR FRENCH FRED

What was it that sent French Fred
Shuddering through the fifth-floor glass
To vault naked over the fire escape?

They said later a sunbathing nun
Witnessed him, bloodied, like a high-wire dancer,
Groan and shout French as he broke through and fell.

He was fine when they dropped him off at noon
Sunday after the Black Party. Drugged, yes, but they
Said his high had peaked. He was fine at noon.

His shoulders were so freckled and so wide.
No wiry-hairy-beret-wearing-baguette-consuming
Continental was this expatriate. He appeared American,

He was as well rounded as a Frisbee.
He liked black men almost exclusively.
He did fall for someone who dumped him over Easter.

The attack poodle, one ex-date dubbed Fred—
High-strung in that French way, but harmless.
He had a good job in communications. Did he have HIV?

A terrible car accident, his father told his mother.
Père and soeur discarded his apartment,
Shipped his heteroed ashes back to Paris.

Thirty-three mourners at the memorial, including
Friends of friends of French Fred. No family.
Departing, one man murmured to another, *Air France.*

—His shoulders were so worked, so beautiful, so tensed.

TERROR

Now God's horrors mean the world to you:
the mad dentist with his TRY CHRIST button
pulling teeth from uncute retarded children,
the Chinese woman crushed beneath the IRT
by a schizophrenic cheery in his checkered shirt,
the kitten's Cheshire growl a serenade
that spirals upward like a crooked RNA,
the armless vet and Richard Nixon singing
arm in arm before a flock of runners
all with tumors sleeping behind their brows.
Could you just scream?
Could you fall before the wise policeman
and tell him panic pins you to the sidewalk?
Nope. Our private scourges seldom coincide
and besides, he's helping a pregnant woman up the curb
who's hand in hand with a child who seems unabused.
So then, like a fingersnap,
the horror garden shifts to Carroll Gardens,
where maybe even every Virgin in the yards
would turn her calloused ear your way;
you hear the subway's regular purr
and bluejays who aren't tiny Isaiahs screaming
but just the usual Brooklyn cantata,
the kind of music you could hum to a friend.
There, now. Are you better now?

TRICKSTER VIDEO

Wile E. Coyote, he's crazy, he burns,
bounces, and tears across the canyon, to skid
on the sharp Arizona sand, as if in this gay bar
his terrible pursuit could conquer gravity,
snare the bird and trick the stars. He's so pathetic,
his hunger too original, and after a beer and a half
your eyes go wet for him and you can't laugh—
poor Coyote never gets his man.

Two Olympic gymnasts, clean American boys,
one light, one dark, float across the screen:
in powdery ease they ride the rings,
the horse, the parallel bars; they move
with grace and aim so grim you believe
there's nothing they'd find worth grinning for.
They are completely happy with their shoulders,
they do not sweat or shit, they are that goddamn bird,

they speed away, beep-beep, all attitude.
Flickering west, they leave you peels of dust.
They are the poultry you were born to die for,
that Wile E. Coyote was born to live for.
And hey! Coyote stands beside you in a muscle tee,
scratching the stubble on his haggard chest.
He drinks a beer like no tomorrow.
He eats you up with his persistent eyes.

Apart together in the light of morning,
your shadows squirm like one against the wall.
He steals off sheepish, without a good-bye kiss.
It's apparent you are not the perfect bird.
He believes with his jet-propelled elastic band
he'll sate himself—today. You feel his fur burn.
Like you, he'll scorch himself, his weary miracle
to recover, to burn and recover and burn.

BIRTHING

I saw a calf's placenta once,
in Scotland, while I was waiting
to rent a horse.

It was bright red, long, and narrow;
it lay on the grass by a fence
like a wet shirt.

All I could think of was
it looked like skin inside out,
as if that sad

thirteen-year-old horse named Guinevere
had nuzzled my teeth, decided
she liked my smell

and put her mouth in my mouth—
like a lion tamer—and dived
all the way down and bitten

and lifted her head up with my skin
with all the force of a swimming woman
shaking the hair from her eyes.

RON'S BEEN DEAD FOUR YEARS

It's as if he never lived, said Dan,
and that was two years ago, and though
Dan is the kind of man who's cleaned his plate
before you've even picked up your fork,
his comment startled and angered me,
as if Ron were a sitcom lasting only several seasons.
But I could not prove Dan otherwise.
Even Ron's voice which I thought as sure
and recurrent as a siren or Ella Fitzgerald
decays into static, like my phone when,
hungry, I stray into the kitchen,
the connection sliced and diced
by appliances and wires hissing in the walls.
His body's as gone as bodies can be,
steel-casketed in some Ohio cemetery
I will never make a point to visit,
though I like the way graveyards level you,
let you feel a part of something bigger,
like gay volleyball. Ron's casket
is a closet, horizontally speaking.
(Ben sewed some pearls into his pants pocket
which his parents, pink and afraid,
will never know about, unless they read poetry.)
But he's not about to jiggle the knob.
Blond old Ron—sweet, deceptively smart,
a fox in cocker spaniel's clothing—
treaded lightly in the world,

less a food than a spice
that nourishes less than it
pauses on the tongue.
He did not grip us;
he ran his fingers down our spine.
He exists in his vanishing like his blondness
in extreme sunlight, in the molecules
of sweat embedded in my mattress
I threw out when Clay moved in, in the *Times*
crossword puzzle we completed
in bed ten months before the toxo took him,
his capital letters distinctively serifed.
Though we uncoupled in July of 1990—
I was impatient with his chuckles, his deliberate *lope*—
I feel sometimes he is mine, that I'm
the spinster scraping birdshit off the statue
of William Cullen Bryant.
What a grandiose and fearful puss I am.
The dead belong to the living blah blah blah.
It's the kind of ownership an adolescent
possesses over Bobby Sherman in the dark.
Ron's gone, dead, canceled,
the rubber of his sneakers scraped on certain pavement
sure to be replaced, his voice alive
in the shape of the streetcorner that he loitered on,
waiting for me, who am late as usual.

MEMORY

A screen door slammed all one summer.

Mrs. Walters's door next door, the summer
in Baltimore I was four, or seven. It slammed
and slammed on its spring, three times each time,
a taut plucked string that finally quiets down.

She bobbed in the netted smoke of the screen.
Did her body float?
No, her slippers scratched the floor.
The screen door

shut how many years? all one summer.

Every herb in my grandfather's garden
stings with the crash, rash, ash of that damned door.
I drop to my knees on the slate in the garden
eye to eye with a bee the size . . . the size
of the stub of my grandfather's cigar.

Listen, hear the hiss of bee
when the mottled screen door eases shut.

Is it wind that eases and hisses all these years?
But Mrs. Walters, you're dead by now,
the neighborhood's changed; look, dead grandpa—
the bumblebee on your stalk of rosemary—
she's sinking of her own rich weight.

DAISY BUCHANAN, 1985

The estate a mile away and long since sold,
The garden ploughed, the house now level ground,
She supposes just the bay remains the same
And knows that even it has changed: Boats, like cars, exist
As smaller crafts of pleasure now, and in the mist
That veils Connecticut, tankers oil the Sound.
In the dayroom, as the other patients play some game—
Coarser women, whose breasts, she notes, lie low—
She glances to her lap and finds she holds
The weekly hand of her daughter in her hand,
Whose face is the earnest annoying white of the moon.
The window admits a shaft of sunlight and
She's warm (though she would never let them know);
She half remembers certain green and linen afternoons.

She remembers one green and linen afternoon—
It must have been last summer—when
They let her stay in bed till noon, and then
Parked her in the sun on the home's front lawn; soon
She felt supremely comfortable, iced tea in one hand,
Watching the traffic light on Western Street
Turn like a leaf from green to yellow, red to green again.
The breeze felt pleasant and the drink was sweet.
But that was years ago. Or days, whatever.

When Pammy wheels her to her room the sun, blunt gold,
Gleams east into her eyes; an orchid on the bedstand
Bends like a butler to greet her, with his single purple vein.
She thinks, I am an orchid. No, a craft of pleasure.
The estate was years ago. It's long since sold.

JOHN BEYOND

These days my friends keep on living,
which used to be odd.
Now it's as common as comb-overs.
I'm out of the habit of obits for breakfast
which goes to show what you can miss
when you fail to be anxious.

Reader, John was my friend
when Ford reigned and Frampton sang.
Now he is newsprint.
Reader, his wrists,
oh his wrists, riotous with hair,
alive on the steering wheel
of the avocado Buick Skylark
as we cruised home from Hackensack
after *Godfather 1*! Or 2!
A man peed right in the street that night:
John howled in a tone I don't recall.
Days or years later in a voice
I don't recall he told me he had just one ball,
which I believe I beheld in a dorm room,
the image now filmy as a vid cap.
That voice, whose every whisper I savored—
Reader, why can't I hear it, when Johnny Carson
resounds in my skull like John Belushi screaming?

John's teeth exhaling smoke, Cameron's nipple,
Brandt's split fingernail, a genital
(Ron's penis floppy pink beneath the hospital gown
or Adi's, jumpy), Kiki's fallen hair,
a hole in Anna's throat, Jay's umber eye askew,
Grandmother's nostrils:
Reader, I cannot detail you to round them up.
My memory descends to the sum of parts
I grope as if in a bar's back room
where the urge to palpate the past is like a lust,
where it's all in the lips, in the wail, in the wrist.

THE CRABMEAT PICKERS

The crab pickers work in nothing like luxury.
After a day and a half the Chesapeake thrill
gives way to a numbness in the wrists that spreads
upward into the shoulders and neck.
But how quick they are, how easily beautiful.
The older woman's carcasses arc out
to a crate that heaps with gleaming gills and eyes.
Her daughter's skin is shining;
the tiny beads on her neck have turned
the color of the farthest water.
They've long since returned the fact of the bay
to its own element,
turning their backs, trading their view
for rhythm. For rhythm
if anything shortens the day,
and the every-second flip of back-fin into a pail
means money in a pocket. Rhythm means
they pay attention just to what is small
(she wipes away the necklace of sweat),
to what occurs in their hands,
in their fingers inside the intricate shells
that click minutes away, six cents a minute.
All day while they work the bay is off repainting itself,
glowing now with cottages and yachts, providing
them with the raw material and a choppy beat,
an odd crabbed pulse of beauty they refine to true detail.

SYMPATHY, 1967

The next-to-last white kid,
he scurries home from school bent over, fast—
Lamont kicked him hard in the pants.
Who won the riots down the street last summer?
Dad says nobody wins riots.
Kids and teacher say, us.

He hides in the ivy that chokes the church.
Last summer somebody flung a brick
through the sacristy window, somebody
swiped his bike from the yard, and Dad
forgave them fast. When the street seems safe
he ventures to the chain link fence
to watch out for Dad, wafting home
from pastoral calls, in that thumb of a Ford
he should trade in for a Barracuda.

A Negro woman in high heels
sways from the Acme supermarket
toward him, buffeted by traffic,
her black pants taut along her hips.
Her glasses arrow into points like hearts.
When he finds her lips they are two glued jewels.
He feels her bare hand fall on the hot white roof of her Corvair.

NEAR RELATIONS

The wind pulls the pollen from the grass, it shouts
so loud I'll never sleep; it raps on the glass to announce
the continent tosses, troubled.
                              A boy feels the sun
on his eyelids as it glints in the east off the mud.
The mat pinched his back all night; the longed-for
rain fell through the roof
and swelled the stitched reeds.
His head stirs. You can see

how his neck is nearly as thin as his arms,
his skin the rich wet color of the ground
that so far grows nothing, though his father
claims it is of great promise.

On the east coast of America my parents try to sleep;
my mother leans restless against my father's back,
my father lies on his side and feels his breathing shorten.

• • •

Sonora, Calcutta, outside Khartoum:
in all these places a boy awakens.
(He wakes as you read this, wherever you are.)
For me at this hour he steps
into Sudanese sunlight, pulling on the striped pants
the Peace Corps left behind. Today
I held Anna in my arms as she cried
into the sleeve of her Fair Isle sweater.

She believes no one has ever actually loved her.
Is she awake too, like the boy?
She's probably twisting her fist in the quilt.

The boy with the black hair and black eyes,
the Sudanese boy,
hears his young brother's cry from the hill's other side;
his mother has poured
rare rainwater over his head.

It rained yesterday. Today they'll celebrate rain
and a recent death in the village.

•   •   •

I drank too much coffee tonight, listening
to Doug tell how this morning he stood
on a rise by Lake Macbride, near the place
a man our age drowned thirty years ago.
His body was never recovered. Standing there
with the sun in his eyes, Doug knew
he'd never hear that young guy's voice; he saw
poverty in all he'd discovered,
how his land and time pinned him: he'd die
and be buried and almost certainly grow nameless.
I saw in his hands that this made him afraid.

The boy reaches into a burlap bag marked USA.
He takes out a fistful of grain.
                        Doug might be
still awake, still gnawing on his wrist,
but I make instead what seems an easy choice:
he falls asleep to find Anna

as she takes a last gulp of water
from her bedside glass and passes out to sleep.
She discovers this man chewing on his palm.

A young man and woman are lying naked together
on a sloping Virginia meadow some cattle have cropped.
The wind thickens in the trees, but they don't notice.
When the sleeping couple reach toward each other
my mother's hand falls over my father's belly.

• • •

They are so happy it has rained at last.
His parents laugh and hold each other's hands
as they climb the damp slope back to the shed.
His little sister sways on his mother's hip,
his little brother grips his father's elbow.
The wind is fierce. Oh, suddenly it's easy,
he'd carry his parents' water forever,
or the bag of grain, or weeds for the fire as far
as they asked, even to the other side of the world.

• • •

That other earth stirs
out of my sleeplessness
and my friends find each other.
Do you think they'll attend each other
when the sun glances west again
or when the wind shifts?
Will my father and mother wake for one more day?

I am falling backward into deep water,
the waves cover my throat, my mouth,
water rises to my eyes—

my brother carries a seeping basket
up from the awakened stream.
The little boy with his finger in his mouth,
the girl who plucks and plucks her cotton shirt,
the father and mother moistened by rain,
dip in one by one with cupped hands.
Their hands leak as they bring them to their lips.

THREE

O BROTHER

On the ferry leaving the summer island behind,
on my last crossing, pulling evenly away from the site
where at age 39 I finally grew aware for whole moments
of things having nothing to do with worry,
where fall now deconstructs the dunes,
the ocean aches for its winter meal of beach,
the deer start their trek to near starvation,
and the sun, entangled in cumulus,
turns the ripe October brilliance to a bruise,

it rises from the foreground of Long Island,
hovering before me, a little embarrassing,
like a teacher holding my slicker open—
a man fully grown, all shoulder and forearm,
his features less Jesus than an ur–Wally Cleaver,
grinning like Buddha, but mostly (I prepare myself)
the miscarriage my mother endured before me,
that lost fish of a child released
into the ocean of unhappening,
the puff of smoke that insinuates itself
into its own disappearance and
returns like a promise, like a John F. Kennedy,
like a memory I didn't know I had—
who straddles the bow and says, "Inhale me, David,

ride with me; I am the nugget of each instant,
nothing but knotted cloud, salt spit, and your bad eyes,
my life your breath, your body your buoy—
I toss myself like a baseball straight your way":

O Clara Barton, Aeneas, boy next door,
my Sakajawea, my Rin Tin Tin,
echo in me longer than the blast of the boat whistle,
more than the sun on my tongue or an Anglican prayer,
head ahead of me,
join me with mainland.

ADDISON GROFF CHOOSES THE MINISTRY

Boonesboro, Maryland. August 1937

On That Tree He Died for Me, O Sacred Head—
they sing the old camp favorites into early evening.
His father, bald head slick with sweat,
steps onto a tree stump. Even the birds grow quiet.
With his back to the sun he opens his mouth.
The faithful, stiff in their holiday shirts,
squint to see him. His shadow flickers on their faces,
lingers on the faces of their children.

•   •   •

At the rise in Wheeler's meadow, Addison
hears just male and female voices,
some tired, some in tune.
Then one speaking.
But now the meadow belongs to him,
an elm, three thick cows,
and a dog who bounds at every diving bird.
For his father a bird's not a bird
but wren, dove, raven, hawk,
each with its bird guide call.
For him the birds make just one sound.

A finger of the bluegrass slips
inside his shirt and he sways,
lips parted: Before him, the sun

singes the top of the elm
at the corner of the pale cornfield,

each hot leaf a bird
singing straight across
the air to him, and when
he shakes his hair from his eyes
the tree limbs glisten
as if the sun stroked out their juice—
the elm arches its back and hisses,
nodding, a body
he, the sun, had touched.

• • •

Sun, elm, leaf.
Addison sits with his chin on his knees
watching the dog and cattle move off
on the path that takes them home,
while the elm thickens in the failing sun

and soon the renewed voices begin to spread
like evening into the meadow, briskly singing,
and smoke from the fires rises
with the scent of grilled corn
and the voice of his father calling.

LAUNDRY

All week long I've been waking afraid,
in the shower fighting the idea of tears
I blot into dampness with a half-stale towel.
After the cheapest possible coffee
I walk through the cold to my friend Steve's,
with his word processor writing chipper letters to employers—
Let me tell you further what I could accomplish for your company—
while in the living room lies Steve's roommate Chuck,
31 years old and eighty-nine pounds, demented and dying,
planning for Florida.

Hey, I'm just a bowl of woes:
Mark the next-to-last lover stumbles around his house,
all his edges blunted, his sighs no longer even histrionic,
the irked cliché retreating to his pantry,
nipping at brandy, sniffing at crystal;
and Jess my young lesbian had cancer cut from her breast—
by Christmas she will lose her fertility and hair
and the hard-ass doctor himself nearly cried
when she asked if she could freeze her eggs before treatment
(she could not; the hormones required conspire with cancer).
Her voice is full of cheerful fear.
No holiday wonder I awake with the edge of sadness that—silly me—
I think is mine alone, my private port wine stain.

• • •

In the task of laundry nothing lasts.
The week's debris stuffed into pillowcases,
the bags hauled down to the laundry room—
like hunger and lust, the need comes back.
I stand glad for the invention of these polluting machines,
almost reliable, and easier than rubbing cloth on the river rocks,
as I wait for some stretch-pantsed woman to finish
in *all six* machines several families' worth of laundry.
Where did she come from? she is not our class dear,
no resident of this upwardly homo building,
but she smiles a shrug. Some days, doing laundry is her job.

I pair the holey socks and fold the underwear, soothe the aging elastics,
the undershirts shrunken to belly length, hardened stains beneath the arms,
the bandannas faded from black to gray and lavender,
the jeans slowly shredding, caught on nails, seat and knees worn smooth,
the tees that flash FLORIDA and the easily swallowed slogan:
ALL I WANT IS A CURE AND MY FRIENDS BACK.
The sheets, their flannel stained and pilled,
I wrestled on with Trevor after he
tore off this black shirt and held me,
mystery bear that he is, all bulk and claw.
He wakes alongside me some mornings,
his sour breath reminding my ear we live.

All of it as clean as it gets.
Each set of briefs
and socks another day that I am scheduled to awake.
Expecting to be soiled, each fragment of fabric is ready
to layer me as I walk and walk my sidewalks,
to blot Chuck's sweat, wipe Mark's lip,
get lent to Trevor and not returned, enturban Jess's cueball skull.
Rags and riches. Armor. Succor.

HOSPITAL GARBAGE, 1968

The brothers are sure they see a liver shift
in a plastic bag too thick to lift:
Inside, they know for sure, lies
all that you could die without—stomachs, hearts.
Or else a whitened eye or cut-off finger,
ear, or tongue—the body's castoff parts
useless now, like an umbilical cord.
The boys jump into the garbage on a silent dare.
They rip the plastic with their fingernails.

A cleaning rag, a shock of gray-blond hair,
a get-well card from Joan, a ball of clothes,
a mirror, panties, a broken dinner tray,
a rosary, red clippings from a lady's toes—
all dull as home. They dig out a crumpled rose
the shade of the black man they saw wheeled in:
His blood bloomed on his scalp, frothed
like spit near his mouth, and sputtered on his chin.
What's real are the rose and the black man's cries.

It was better to imagine trash. They linger,
hoping for a brain, a baby's lung, or just a bloody cloth
to carry home and handle, think about, inhale—
something scary, stinky, and worth stealing.

Evening turns the smells and colors gray.
They head home for supper hungry, tired, and bored,
to wash their hands and faces badly, feeling
cheated somehow. Still, they feel a sneaky power—
in each boy's pocket petals of the black man's flower.

LIFE MASK OF TOM

If I had lowered his mask
over the wasted face of his death
he could still have breathed
if he could have breathed.
While I snore safely into his ear,
Doug might grab him off the nightstand
and eye to seam of eye recall
the contours he has memorized:
the brow upset, downcast,
mouth too taut to admit a breath,
the open nostrils tiny oases.
Once Doug woke to find Tom gone.
Out in the street, in heavy rain,
he found him, wandering at dawn.
Tom saw him and started walking faster.
Doug caught up and grabbed his hand.
Tom turned, a scary brightness in his eyes.
"I must go to a party in Doug's home,"
he explained. "It's in my brain."
If grief could irrigate his face—or fear—
then Tom would bloom. He'd rearrange
his grimace for us. But his face is
saying only, You two are there, I'm here.
I could hang Tom like an icon on the wall
but he'd still be a burglar breaking in,
his opinion of us muffled by the plaster.
I flip him face down by the bedside phone,

rocking gently on his nose and chin,
and mix in the dry cavern of his head
the contents of our pockets
when Doug and I undress for bed:
a safety pin, my contacts,
a condom, keys, and change.

YOUR HEADACHE

lay in no vault I could inhabit
or even visit
like a cottage in a storm,
weighing with one palm
the wind against the walls.
You lay on the gurney
rapt in your body,

eyes scorched shut
in the heat of your pain.
Every touch of mine hurt.
Sick of standing, I went
to crouch beside you,
my chin on your mattress,
but my knee hurt.

My knee hurt so badly
I thought it would give
under me, snap
like some shot lark
who knows simply
pain and the sensation
of drop drop drop

with no notion why it falls
or how to right itself,
its brain too blunt
to know it dies
but tumbling now,
entirely gravity,
to the kiss of impact.

THE WATCHDYKE

For Eric and Peter

When you walk holding hands into a sea so cold
your thighs give way and you go instantly numb,
she swims between your calves and nips your ankles,
her body a jetty that undoes the undertow.
She howls, you spin around, too late to catch her squint
through driftwood at how silly you can be,
flapping your arms like the free, dumb
gulls who grace the fishing boats all day
in flea-market glee (she mimics them in Portuguese).
As you fall asleep she stands above your forms
to keep the sun from searing your nude faces,
then groans like a whale to start you both awake,
and, sandpiper-nimble, scoots behind a dune
to hoot at you. When you begin to climb
(so weary) up the dunes and down again,
past the single beech, the minnow pool,
toward the road that takes you home—
the road with its sports cars wide-awake and savage—
you see her footsteps in the sand before you,
webbed and deep and made for you to walk in.
Porpoise, seagull, St. Bernard, she runs ahead of you—you
with all your gear, your heat, your breathlessness.

NAMING CONSTELLATIONS

My father and I are walking the flat land toward Horsey's Pond.
The sky's like the inside of a shell, he says,
the stars are salt.
I've read the *Child's Guide to Stars* but forgot them all.
He says, Remember.

"That's Orion over there walking like an Indian,
in single file, the sticks of corn are the Apollo twins—
see them? don't they look like corn?—
there's Phoebe in his chariot
driving Mr. Wheeler's horses on the sky
and, you know, when he rides too close to the Bear he falls,
the sky comes crashing down on us—"

I look up at his lighted face.
Does he believe me? Big old man, if you wanted
you could toss me over your shoulder for luck.

He looks up at me, then up at the sky.

He nods! My father nods!
Like the grass beneath our feet or the fence posts
we rest against when my voice slows him down,
my story's true—

I sway on his hands, playing, naming stars
until I'm the best of the child liars, ten, inventing
constellations out of birds, squirrels, snakes.
But I run out of animals. His neck gets tired.
He puts my hand in his pocket and takes me home.

We take a long time going home, the long way,
passing underneath the pond's broad trees
and across Mr. Wheeler's where the horses graze.
We're quiet, both of us, the whole way home.
We're thinking about the stars, how we
named them, how they don't know their own names.

FOR CATCHING HARDSHELL CRABS

The chicken is so ripe
it's an agony to smell it and tie it on the line.
Tie it tight, three times, so the crab
can't sneak it off without you knowing.
Then lower it in the water,
the deepest water underneath the dock,
so slowly your fingers tremble.
The string goes slack: stop.
You wait. Wait a long time, sometimes.
You feel the tug—there's your crab
toying with your bait, his food.
Let him get a good grip
on that ripe old leg, then pull him up,
hand over hand, like bringing in a kite,
except that this is water.
Your crab will drop back down
if he gets bored or understands—
but if he hangs on, if you
have done this well, you'll see him,
greener than the water.
When you've eased him up,
grab the catcher's net, lunge,
cut off his escape so when he falls
you net him. Don't be surprised
at how surprised he looks.
Drop him in the basket, clamp the top.
Let him think you're water, only dry.

FACING EAST NEAR BIG SUR

The cliffs behind us and their great drop,
The sky an even medicinal blue, and just below it,
The noise of the largest ocean—
I can tell by the twitch in your smile how edgy
The edge makes you, here where all we can do is
Admit how small we are in scale, admire
The coast and maybe wade past it,
Or sit in the rocky sand and finally
Lean back and fall asleep in an outsized landscape
Under a close sun. Maybe life in fact if not in deed
Lasts longer here, thanks to the beauty
That may in fact rub off on us, making the dull
Progress of the body primary, the sun
A name for a kind of contentment;
But instead of all that I'm thinking, lover, of the waves
Who swept across the continent to break
And blunt themselves atop these bluffs,
Their adrenalin still furious, but no new land out there.
I'm thinking how, for now, we need to keep the ocean
At our backs and revisit the china closets
Abandoned on the frozen Mormon Handcart Trail,
The transcendental writing desks in Pennsylvania barns—
Go back along the route they took before; and if the thrill
Of unfamiliarity is gone from the Rockies and the corn
Looks like corn, if we're part of the ebb, so be it, because
We're grown-ups these days, on personal land.
We choose a city we read in the grain of our faces

And inhabit like the seventh building on this site,
Its terraces more dangerous than cliffs.
And always just beyond us, keeping us awake,
Almost visible at the end
Or start of the line (depending which way we face)
Lies the smaller cool Atlantic, looking forward to us.

THE SENSE OF WELL-BEING

At dusk's inexact instant
the brownstone sounds, the dishes
clicking in kitchens,
the whippet's hollow whine,
a siren, someone's distant Spanish,
disappear into silence
until the street is a hollow thing
beyond all murmuring,
your footsteps as crisp
as a clock. You lack
all recrimination, pure
as traffic-hum, like a bum
who doesn't ask for change,
with all the commerce halted,
all the longing gone.

THE SADDLE RIVER

Like that pipe spilling something black
through the weeds to the Saddle River,
I was the smell in the marsh that crept
beneath the foundation, I seeped through the walls
of the church I sat in dozens of Sunday schools asking
if Jesus did it too, or the organist, or my father.
I hated how my father's clear blue eyes
met my mother's, and the simple way he'd ask at night
what I'd done with myself that day.
God! the breasts that shook the whole way through the park,
the corduroy knee I touched in a movie,
and years the dream where we swam by that pipe,
those boys and me—drowning, repenting everything,
flinging our arms out, out.

Tonight the air clears, the speaking fades
in the other houses, and domestic lights dissolve.
It's so cold by the river the grass crackles as I walk on it.
I am arrested by the shades of summer bodies,
pairs of legs stretched out on the picnic tables
wet and bare, and the dogs who pulled themselves
on their stomachs over the moist lawn, they were so happy.
I've seen how in spring when it rains the water
folds itself over and stirs like a body waking,

how the river smooths its refuse into the grass.
With my eyes closed I can nose out the places
where the cold weeds smell to heaven;
but I hold that in the current, under the ragged oil,
fish find each other, touch, and part.

PERSONAL LAND

For M.

1

New Jersey drives itself to this:
An abandoned car, blurred with snow,
its upholstery cracked, its engine rust,
sinks past its doorlocks in the chemical mud.
For you I dig it out and wipe the toxins off
just to spirit you away from my home,
away from the blizzard that resembles car exhaust,
risking the tire-shredding railroad crossing,
the trucks groaning into gear for the trip west,
the zero-to-sixty.

What would it take to clear the air,
spread us out, give us room?
I'd let Genovese Liquor go—with its California
marble glistening miserably pink in the headlights—
the Cape Cod bank, the stoplights at each block,
the barbershop run by Hardy, an ex-Marine,
and the Sacred Heart glass tower
with its lit Christ scaring the drunks.
If it could all go ahead and fall,
all of it brittle in cold weather,
we could crack the ice and gulp the nasty river down.

2

Lent or something like it
settles on us. You watch the Good Shepherd
shut his glassy eyes in pain.
You two understand each other.
He balances, stained, much like yourself,
dust in his leaded veins,
illuminated from behind for half the day.
The lamb on his arm looks heavy
and he grimaces like the long-ignored;
he lives for Sundays when he meets my father's eyes
at the benediction, and my father nods hello.
At *who did once upon the cross*
suffer to redeem our loss
he trembles with the deafest vestryman
as the crucifer ascends the steps toward God.
When the swollen music and the stained-glass light
make you shiver with precipitate belief,
over you a jet will wail its way toward Newark,
descending fast across the Palisades
to ruffle the gutter grasses of the Meadowlands.
Christ and his lilies shudder and your voice drowns.

3

Dirtbags, my brother calls them.
We walk carefully as ladies among them,
the kids squatting in their cars
or in the doors of their vans, in the county park,
shirtless, smoking, drinking,
expecting nothing but a day like this.
Some cars have a girl in a tube top
laid out on the hood like a mascot

but I've seen some other women saunter
or stumble from one car to another,
looking for guys they know.

Ash flicked on the grass.
Another flick a minute later.
No past to talk about
except last April when the cops cracked down.

We cross the river retrenched for Route 80,
to the town where they named the treeless streets after trees
and after the town's dead corporals and privates.
What a place for you to re-enter the world,
with all the bulky fathers
beholding their lawns as if lawns talked back,
the kids who nearly run you over
as they leap into their Camaros
escaping on the trip "down shore."
The aluminum siding is hot to touch
and wherever you look there is only the present
leaving its dust on the street, the people, the river.
I find you a grassy place behind Wowser's, an old closed bar,
and we stay there, sweating and dirty, a long time.
Michael, my only dirtbag, open your eyes.
If God would roust us like a wise policeman
we'd just sit there in the heat and not believe a word.

4

You have always loved pumpkins.
I place one on your lap.
If you'd asked Atlantic City you'd have got
ten to one on Jersey air,
but the gourd's complete, its appearance normal,
a benign near globe of hollow fruit and seed.

Recall the Indians,
anticipating the hard cold, kicking it open,
eating it, saving its seeds to dry over winter.
Imagine a Paterson family dropping a pumpkin
to split it into slices,
talking Spanish in the asphalt courtyard.
Hear the sound that arises,
like ice cracking or a brain bursting.

5

Have I been too depressing?
I speed through Lodi on my way to the supermarket
wishing not for any Advent but for gratitude,
that I could be glad to be sobered,
pleased for the boys in their depreciating cars,
glad I worry for you as well, and glad
that the women are heading to Sacred Heart for bingo
(tonight more than one will win something).

I think the trick of resurrection
is to the see the soil as embraceable,
no matter where it falls—on new snow,
on the hot hoods of cars, even on your face.
As you and I embrace, dirty as we are.
No matter how much we foul ourselves,
how much grass churns underneath our wheels
or how many fish the ocean coughs,
we are only partly our pollution.

Oh, I can describe Santa Claus on the lime-colored
fire truck Christmas Eve, handing down the candy cane,
ho-ho-ho over the bullhorn.
I can depress you again or make you angry by telling
how local thugs repeatedly slammed one nelly kid

against the barber pole until his head was bleeding.
I can make you sick with a story
of river rats edging up from the frozen brook whose stink
the children splash in every summer.
But in my fear and my anger
remember the members of my father's congregation
at midnight services when they kneel for the newborn baby:
The acolyte flicks off the lights, and they sing.

MAGNITUDES

Consider Mayo's chuckle,
its breadth so small
compared to the sounding
of even this mild ocean,
making its minimal waves break
on unshielded shore.
Is it wave, salt, wind
or molecule that rips
the beach apart?
Inside us, inside the wave,
inside the men who dredge the dunes
looking for decent action, dwells
the catalytic tide—
a jellyfish dead, its burden of sting
ejected like a sigh into the foam,
a poison defused,
sent off humbled by the kidney,
the germ (a word too bad, too big,
less specific than a sea)
whose duties cure cheese,
ease bowels, cause blood
to flow or die; the seed
we breathe in like a stranger's sneeze
until from wind, wave, and molecule,
like all of Fire Island we erode,
a sandbar lessened into sand
the water easily absconds with, and

the very premise of shore,
the largest iota around,
gives way to wave,
and we become the ocean floor.
In the silence between two breakers
Mayo laughs, loud.

ILLINOIS POETRY SERIES

Laurence Lieberman, Editor

The American Book of the Dead
Jim Barnes (1982)

The Floating Candles
Sydney Lea (1982)

Northbook
Frederick Morgan (1982)

Collected Poems, 1930–83
Josephine Miles (1983; reissue, 1999)

The River Painter
Emily Grosholz (1984)

Healing Song for the Inner Ear
Michael S. Harper (1984)

The Passion of the Right-Angled Man
T. R. Hummer (1984)

Dear John, Dear Coltrane
Michael S. Harper (1985)

Poems from the Sangamon
John Knoepfle (1985)

In It
Stephen Berg (1986)

The Ghosts of Who We Were
Phyllis Thompson (1986)

Moon in a Mason Jar
Robert Wrigley (1986)

Lower-Class Heresy
T. R. Hummer (1987)

Poems: New and Selected
Frederick Morgan (1987)

Furnace Harbor: A Rhapsody of the
    North Country
Philip D. Church (1988)

Bad Girl, with Hawk
Nance Van Winckel (1988)

Blue Tango
Michael Van Walleghen (1989)

Eden
Dennis Schmitz (1989)

Waiting for Poppa at the Smithtown Diner
Peter Serchuk (1990)

Great Blue
Brendan Galvin (1990)

What My Father Believed
Robert Wrigley (1991)

Something Grazes Our Hair
S. J. Marks (1991)

Walking the Blind Dog
G. E. Murray (1992)

The Sawdust War
Jim Barnes (1992)

The God of Indeterminacy
Sandra McPherson (1993)

Off-Season at the Edge of the World
Debora Greger (1994)

Counting the Black Angels
Len Roberts (1994)

Oblivion
Stephen Berg (1995)

NATIONAL POETRY SERIES

Eroding Witness
Nathaniel Mackey (1985)
Selected by Michael S. Harper

Palladium
Alice Fulton (1986)
Selected by Mark Strand

Cities in Motion
Sylvia Moss (1987)
Selected by Derek Walcott

The Hand of God and a Few
   Bright Flowers
William Olsen (1988)
Selected by David Wagoner

The Great Bird of Love
Paul Zimmer (1989)
Selected by William Stafford

Stubborn
Roland Flint (1990)
Selected by Dave Smith

The Surface
Laura Mullen (1991)
Selected by C. K. Williams

The Dig
Lynn Emanuel (1992)
Selected by Gerald Stern

My Alexandria
Mark Doty (1993)
Selected by Philip Levine

The High Road to Taos
Martin Edmunds (1994)
Selected by Donald Hall

Theater of Animals
Samn Stockwell (1995)
Selected by Louise Glück

The Broken World
Marcus Cafagña (1996)
Selected by Yusef Komunyakaa

Nine Skies
A. V. Christie (1997)
Selected by Sandra McPherson

Lost Wax
Heather Ramsdell (1998)
Selected by James Tate

So Often the Pitcher Goes to Water
   until It Breaks
Rigoberto González (1999)
Selected by Ai

Renunciation
Corey Marks (2000)
Selected by Philip Levine

Manderley
Rebecca Wolff (2001)
Selected by Robert Pinsky

Theory of Devolution
David Groff (2002)
Selected by Mark Doty

OTHER POETRY VOLUMES

Local Men and Domains
James Whitehead (1987)

Her Soul beneath the Bone: Women's
Poetry on Breast Cancer
Edited by Leatrice Lifshitz (1988)

Days from a Dream Almanac
Dennis Tedlock (1990)

Working Classics: Poems on Industrial Life
Edited by Peter Oresick and Nicholas Coles
(1990)

Hummers, Knucklers, and Slow Curves:
Contemporary Baseball Poems
Edited by Don Johnson (1991)

The Double Reckoning of Christopher
Columbus
Barbara Helfgott Hyett (1992)

Selected Poems
Jean Garrigue (1992)

New and Selected Poems, 1962–92
Laurence Lieberman (1993)

The Dig and Hotel Fiesta
Lynn Emanuel (1994)

For a Living: The Poetry of Work
Edited by Nicholas Coles and Peter Oresick
(1995)

The Tracks We Leave: Poems on
Endangered Wildlife of North America
Barbara Helfgott Hyett (1996)

Peasants Wake for Fellini's Casanova and
Other Poems
Andrea Zanzotto; edited and translated by
John P. Welle and Ruth Feldman;
drawings by Federico Fellini and Augusto
Murer (1997)

Moon in a Mason Jar and What My
Father Believed
Robert Wrigley (1997)

The Wild Card: Selected Poems,
Early and Late
Karl Shapiro; edited by Stanley Kunitz and
David Ignatow (1998)

Turtle, Swan and Bethlehem in Broad
Daylight
Mark Doty (2000)

Illinois Voices: An Anthology of Twentieth-
Century Poetry
Edited by Kevin Stein and G. E. Murray
(2001)

On a Wing of the Sun
Jim Barnes (3-volume reissue, 2001)

Poems
William Carlos Williams; introduction by
Virginia M. Wright-Peterson (2002)

The University of Illinois Press
is a founding member of the
Association of American University Presses.

———————————————————————

Composed in 10.5/14 Minion
with Meta display
by Jim Proefrock
at the University of Illinois Press
Designed by Dennis Roberts
Manufactured by Thomson-Shore, Inc.

University of Illinois Press
1325 South Oak Street
Champaign, IL 61820-6903
www.press.uillinois.edu